06 C156.19

W9-BGD-544

FACTS AND FIGURES

PLANETS

Nancy Dickmann

WINDMILL
BOOKS

Published in 2019 by **Windmill Books**, an imprint of Rosen Publishing
29 East 21st Street, New York, NY 10010

For Brown Bear Books Ltd:
Text and Editor: Nancy Dickmann
Children's Publisher: Anne O'Daly
Editorial Director: Lindsey Lowe
Design Manager: Keith Davis
Designer and Illustrator: Supriya Sahai
Picture Manager: Sophie Mortimer

Concept development: Square and Circus/Brown Bear Books Ltd

Picture Credits:
Front cover: Supriya Sahai
Interior: NASA: 22–23, Ames/JPL-Caltech 29b, ESA 28-29, JPL 8–9, 15, 18, 28, JPL-Caltech 27,
JPL-Caltech/Space Science Institute 16, JPL-Caltech/UCLA/MPS/DLR/IDA 25, JPL/Space
Science Insititute 23, JSC 9; Shutterstock: 3drenderings 19, adike 11, Alhovik 5, By 17, 29t,
Pavel Chagochkin 12, Andrea Danti 10, DeymosHR 14, Dotted Yeti 6, 13, 22, Elenarts 8, NASA 7,
SergeyDV 4, Tristan3D 21.

Key: t=top, b=bottom, c=center, l=left, r=right

Brown Bear Books has made every attempt to contact the copyright holder.
If anyone has any information please contact licensing@brownbearbooks.co.uk

Cataloging-in-Publication Data

Names: Dickmann, Nancy.
Title: Planets / Nancy Dickmann.
Description: New York : Windmill Books, 2019. | Series: Space facts and figures |
Includes glossary and index.
Identifiers: LCCN ISBN 9781508195191 (pbk.) | ISBN 9781508195184 (library bound) |
ISBN 9781508195207 (6 pack)
Subjects: LCSH: Planets--Juvenile literature.
Classification: LCC QB602.D53 2019 | DDC 523.4--dc23

Manufactured in the United States of America

CPSIA Compliance Information: Batch #BS18WM:
For Further Information contact Rosen Publishing, New York, New York at 1-800-237-9932

CONTENTS

WHAT IS A PLANET?

A planet is a large body that goes around the sun. There are eight planets in our solar system.

Not all planets are the same. Some are big, and some are smaller. Some are made of rock, and others of gases. Six of the planets have one or more **moons**. Only one planet has plants and animals living on it. This is Earth—our home.

Mars Rover

Robots have landed on two planets to explore: Venus and Mars.

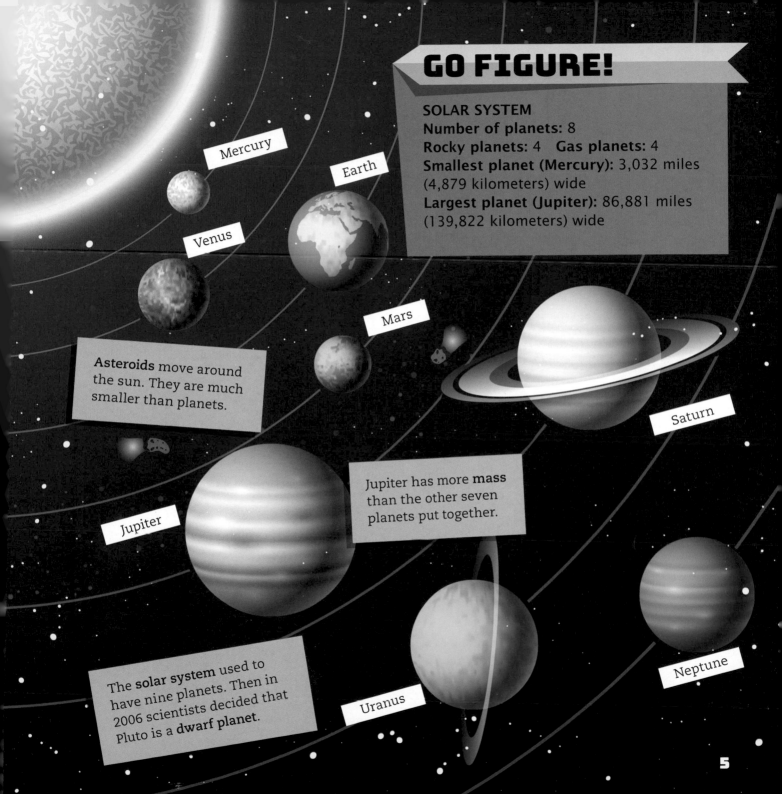

GO FIGURE!

Mercury

Earth

Venus

Mars

Saturn

Asteroids move around the sun. They are much smaller than planets.

Jupiter has more **mass** than the other seven planets put together.

Jupiter

The **solar system** used to have nine planets. Then in 2006 scientists decided that Pluto is a **dwarf planet**.

Uranus

Neptune

MERCURY

**Mercury is the smallest planet.
It is also the closest one to the sun.**

Mercury is rocky, and its surface is covered in **craters**. The craters were made when other objects smashed into Mercury. Mercury has very little **atmosphere** to protect it from impacts. The side of Mercury that faces the sun gets very hot. The side that is in darkness is much colder.

Mercury travels around the sun faster than any other planet.

Mercury's largest crater is about 963 miles (1,550 kilometers) wide.

There is ice deep inside some of Mercury's craters.

Mercury is only slightly larger than Earth's moon.

Metal **core**

Underneath the rocky surface, Mercury is made of metal.

GO FIGURE!

Diameter: 3,032 miles (4,879 kilometers)
Number of moons: 0
Average distance from sun: 35,983,125 miles (57,909,227 kilometers)
Length of day: 59 Earth days
Length of year: 88 Earth days
Hottest temperature: 801 ˚Fahrenheit (427 ˚Celsius)
Coldest temperature: –279 ˚Fahrenheit (–173 ˚Celsius)

VENUS

Venus is rocky, like Earth, and it is similar in size. But the two planets are very different. You wouldn't want to live on Venus!

Venus is covered in a thick blanket of clouds. They trap the sun's heat so the planet is extremely hot. Beneath the clouds are **volcanoes**, valleys, and highlands. Most of the planet's surface is covered in **lava** from volcanic eruptions.

Magellan probe

More than 40 spacecraft have explored Venus.

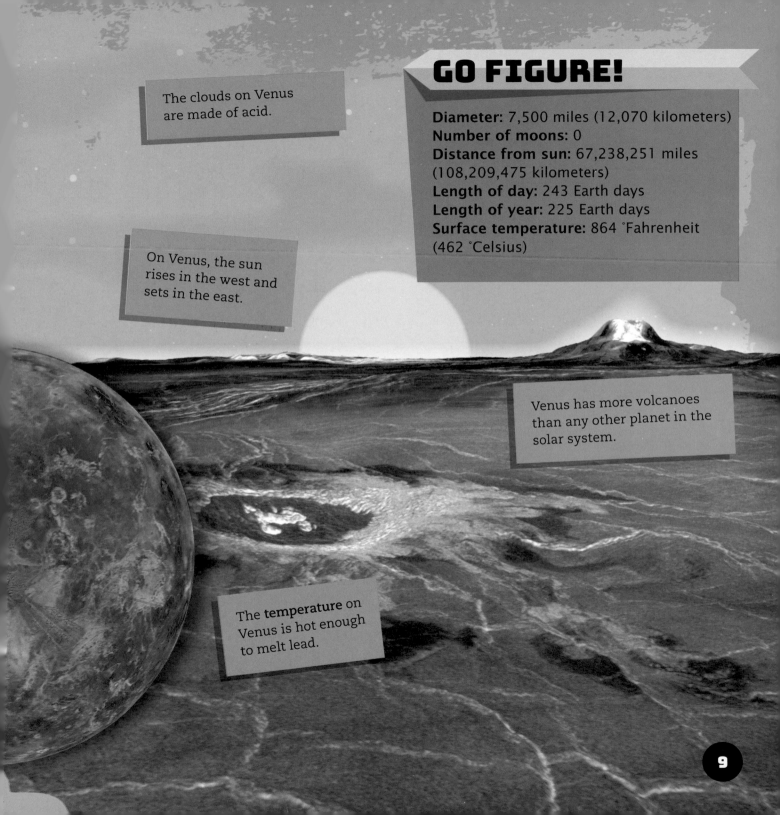

The clouds on Venus are made of acid.

GO FIGURE!

Diameter: 7,500 miles (12,070 kilometers)
Number of moons: 0
Distance from sun: 67,238,251 miles (108,209,475 kilometers)
Length of day: 243 Earth days
Length of year: 225 Earth days
Surface temperature: 864 °Fahrenheit (462 °Celsius)

On Venus, the sun rises in the west and sets in the east.

Venus has more volcanoes than any other planet in the solar system.

The **temperature** on Venus is hot enough to melt lead.

EARTH

Our home planet is the third from the sun. It is the largest of the four rocky planets. It is the fifth largest overall.

Earth is sometimes called the "blue planet." Water in the oceans makes Earth look blue from space. No other planet has liquid water on its surface. Earth has an atmosphere made of gases. The atmosphere protects us from harmful rays from the sun. It keeps the temperature from getting too hot or cold.

Earth is the only planet with an atmosphere that humans can breathe.

Earth's atmosphere protects us from all but the largest space rocks.

It takes about 8 minutes for light from the sun to reach Earth.

Earth is made of four layers.

Crust

Mantle

Outer core

Inner core

There are more than 8 million types of living things on Earth.

GO FIGURE!

Diameter: 7,918 miles (12,742 kilometers)
Number of moons: 1
Distance from sun: 92,956,050 miles (149,598,262 kilometers)
Length of day: 24 hours
Length of year: 365 days
Hottest temperature: 136 °Fahrenheit (58 °Celsius)
Coldest temperature: –126 °Fahrenheit (–88 °Celsius)

MARS

Mars is called the red planet. It is now a rocky desert, but it may have once been more like Earth. There might even have been life on Mars a long time ago!

Mars is a rocky planet that is smaller than Earth. Water once flowed across its surface. Long ago, Mars had an atmosphere like Earth's. Now its atmosphere is very thin. Over billions of years, the **solar wind** stripped away Mars's atmosphere. The planet grew cold, and its liquid water disappeared.

Many people think that one day we will build homes on Mars.

The polar **ice caps** on Mars are made of water ice and frozen **carbon dioxide**.

Martian north pole

Mars's two moons may be asteroids that were captured by its **gravity**.

GO FIGURE!

Diameter: 4,212 miles (6,779 kilometers)
Number of moons: 2
Distance from sun: 141,637,725 miles (227,943,824 kilometers)
Length of day: 24.6 Earth hours
Length of year: 687 Earth days
Hottest temperature: 70 °Fahrenheit (20 °Celsius)
Coldest temperature: –225 °Fahrenheit (–153 °Celsius)

There is a huge volcano on Mars called Olympus Mons. It is three times as tall as Mount Everest.

Mars gets its red color from rust (iron oxide) in the soil.

13

JUPITER

Mighty Jupiter is the king of the planets! It is the largest planet in the solar system. It has the most moons, and it spins the fastest.

Jupiter is made of gas. The stripes that we see on its surface are bands of swirling clouds. Jupiter's appearance changes over time as the clouds move around. The winds on Jupiter are very strong, and there are fierce storms. The famous Great Red Spot is a giant storm about the same size as Earth. It has raged for more than 300 years.

Jupiter spins so fast that it has the shortest day of all the planets.

More than 1,300 Earths could fit into Jupiter!

Jupiter may have a solid core that is about the size of the Earth.

Jupiter is made from the same ingredients as stars, but it is not big enough to shine.

It is named for the king of the Roman gods.

Spacecraft cannot land on Jupiter because there is no solid surface.

Storm

GO FIGURE!

Diameter: 86,881 miles (139,822 kilometers)
Number of moons: at least 69
Distance from sun: 483,638,564 miles (778,340,821 kilometers)
Length of day: 9.9 Earth hours
Length of year: about 12 Earth years
Average temperature: −234 ˚Fahrenheit (−148 ˚Celsius)

SATURN

Saturn is made of gas, like Jupiter. It has more than 60 moons. Saturn has a feature that really makes it stand out: its beautiful system of rings.

Saturn is very light for its size. It would float if it were placed in water!

Saturn's rings were first spotted with a **telescope** about 400 years ago. They are made of chunks of ice and rock. The biggest pieces are the size of a house. The smallest are as tiny as a grain of sand. There are seven separate rings, divided by gaps. Some of Saturn's moons move through these gaps.

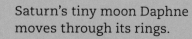

Saturn's tiny moon Daphne moves through its rings.

A chemical called ammonia gives Saturn its yellowish-tan color.

There is a giant hexagon-shaped pattern of winds at Saturn's north pole.

Saturn has seasons.

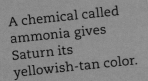

GO FIGURE!

Diameter: 72,367 miles
(116,464 kilometers)
Number of moons: at least 62
Distance from sun: 886,489,415 miles
(1,426,666,422 kilometers)
Length of day: 10.7 Earth hours
Length of year: about 29 Earth years
Average temperature: –288 ˚Fahrenheit
(–178 ˚Celsius)

The Cassini spacecraft has spent years studying Saturn, its rings, and its moons.

URANUS

Uranus is so cold that its gases are more like ice. It lies far from the sun, toward the edge of the solar system. The sun's light and heat hardly reach the planet.

All the planets in the solar system spin around an imaginary line called an **axis**. Some planets' axes are almost straight up and down. Others are tilted slightly. Uranus' axis is tilted so much that the planet is tipped on its side. **Astronomers** think that large objects crashed into Uranus a long time ago. This knocked the planet sideways.

Only one spacecraft, *Voyager 2*, has ever visited Uranus.

Uranus was the first planet to be discovered by using a telescope, in 1781.

Diameter: 31,518 miles (50,724 kilometers)
Number of moons: 27
Distance from sun: 1,783,744,300 miles (2,870,658,186 kilometers)
Length of day: 17 Earth hours
Length of year: 84 Earth years
Average temperature: –357 ˚Fahrenheit (–216 ˚Celsius)

Deep inside Uranus there is a small rocky core.

Rocky inner core

Uranus has 13 thin rings. They are darker and harder to see than Saturn's rings.

It takes sunlight 2 hours and 40 minutes to reach Uranus.

NEPTUNE

Neptune was discovered in an unusual way. By looking at wobbles in the orbit of Uranus, scientists figured out where the eighth planet would be.

Neptune is the farthest planet from the sun. It is cold and very windy. The winds that tear through Neptune's icy clouds can blow at 1,200 miles (2,000 kilometers) per hour. That is about five times as fast as the most powerful winds on Earth.

Neptune is big enough for 60 Earths to fit inside it.

Earth (average)
61°F (15°C)

Freezer
0°F (–18°C)

Antarctica
–70°F (–57°C)

Neptune (average)
–353°F (–214°C)

Neptune is one of the coldest planets in the solar system.

There used to be a giant storm visible on the surface, but it has disappeared.

The path of Neptune's **orbit** overlaps with that of the dwarf planet Pluto.

GO FIGURE!

Diameter: 30,599 miles
(49,244 kilometers)
Number of moons: 14
Distance from sun: 2,795,173,960 miles
(4,498,396,441 kilometers)
Length of day: 16 Earth hours
Length of year: 165 Earth years
Average temperature: –353 ˚Fahrenheit
(–214 ˚Celsius)

Astronomers predicted where Neptune would be, before it was spotted with a telescope.

Neptune has six rings, but they are very hard to see.

AMAZING MOONS

A moon is an object that orbits a planet, dwarf planet, or asteroid. Most of the planets in the solar system have at least one moon.

In 2005, the spacecraft *Huygens* landed on the surface of Titan.

Europa

Most moons are fairly small, but Jupiter and Saturn each have a moon that is bigger than Mercury! If these moons went around the sun instead of orbiting planets, they would be called planets. Most moons are rocky or icy, or a mixture of the two. Astronomers think that some moons have oceans of liquid water beneath the surface.

Jupiter's moon Europa has a cracked surface made of ice.

Earth's moon

Titan

Ganymede

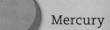
Mercury

Ganymede is the biggest moon in our solar system.

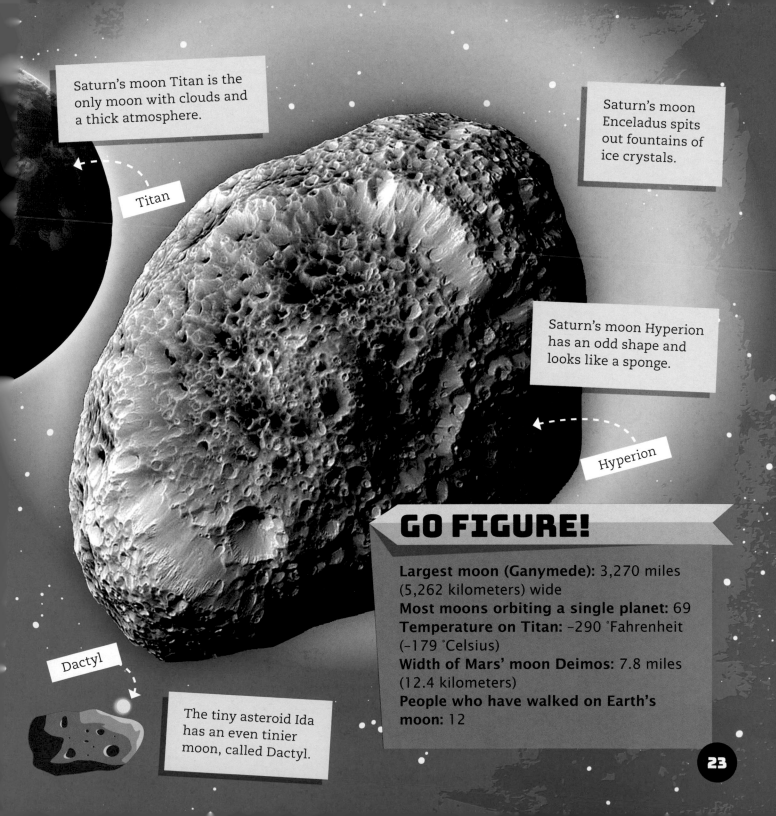

Saturn's moon Titan is the only moon with clouds and a thick atmosphere.

Titan

Saturn's moon Enceladus spits out fountains of ice crystals.

Saturn's moon Hyperion has an odd shape and looks like a sponge.

Hyperion

GO FIGURE!

Largest moon (Ganymede): 3,270 miles (5,262 kilometers) wide
Most moons orbiting a single planet: 69
Temperature on Titan: –290 °Fahrenheit (–179 °Celsius)
Width of Mars' moon Deimos: 7.8 miles (12.4 kilometers)
People who have walked on Earth's moon: 12

Dactyl

The tiny asteroid Ida has an even tinier moon, called Dactyl.

DWARF PLANETS

Dwarf planets travel around the sun. They are smaller than planets but bigger than asteroids.

Our solar system has five dwarf planets. They are Pluto, Ceres, Eris, Makemake, and Haumea. Ceres is the smallest dwarf planet. It was the first one to be discovered. Ceres is the closest dwarf planet to the Sun. It is in the asteroid belt between Mars and Jupiter. The other dwarf planets are in the outer solar system.

Ceres

moon

Ceres is quite small compared to our moon.

Earth

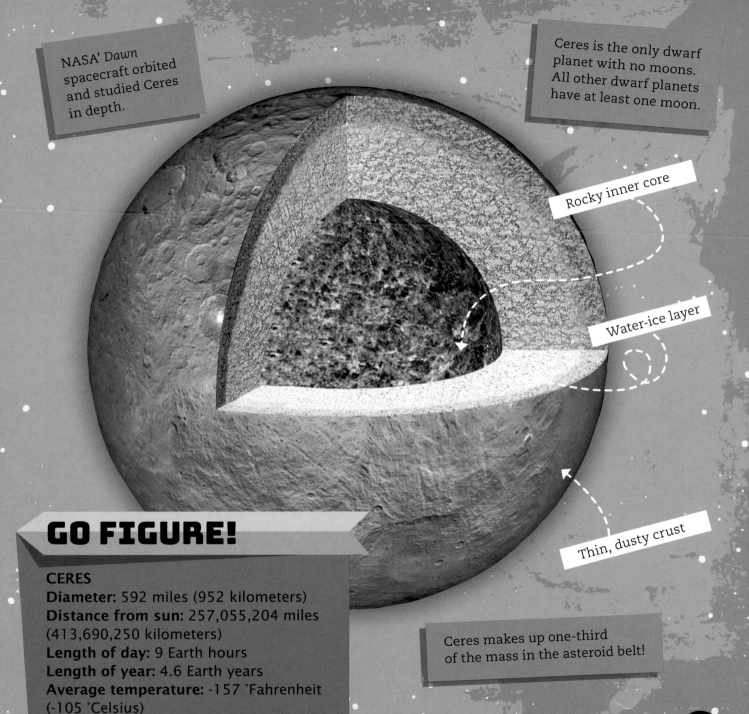

NASA' *Dawn* spacecraft orbited and studied Ceres in depth.

Ceres is the only dwarf planet with no moons. All other dwarf planets have at least one moon.

Rocky inner core

Water-ice layer

Thin, dusty crust

GO FIGURE!

CERES
Diameter: 592 miles (952 kilometers)
Distance from sun: 257,055,204 miles (413,690,250 kilometers)
Length of day: 9 Earth hours
Length of year: 4.6 Earth years
Average temperature: -157 °Fahrenheit (-105 °Celsius)

Ceres makes up one-third of the mass in the asteroid belt!

EXOPLANETS

There are planets in places beyond our solar system. These planets are called exoplanets. They move around a star, just like the planets in our solar system.

The first **exoplanet** moving around a star like our sun was found in 1995. Since then, astronomers have found many more. Some are gas giants, like Jupiter and Saturn. Others are small and rocky. Many astronomers think some of these exoplanets could be home to living things.

Exoplanets that are the right distance from their star might have water on the surface.

Astronomers call this region the "Goldilocks Zone" because it is not too hot and not too cold.

The Kepler Space Telescope has discovered more than 2,300 confirmed exoplanets.

The first exoplanet to be discovered is called 51 Pegasi B.

Astronomers have discovered at least one exoplanet with its own exomoon!

A temporary dip in a star's brightness is a sign that an exoplanet is passing in front of it.

GO FIGURE!

Temperature on 51 Pegasi B: at least 1,832 °Fahrenheit (1,000 °Celsius)
Exoplanets orbiting the star Trappist-1: 7
Farthest exoplanet discovered: 27,710 light-years away
Biggest exoplanet discovered so far: about 29 times the size of Jupiter

QUIZ

Try this quiz and test your knowledge of the planets! The answers are on page 32.

1 What is hiding inside some of Mercury's craters?
A. lava
B. ice
C. cheese

2 What are the clouds on Venus made of?
A. acid
B. cotton balls
C. water

3 What gives Mars its red color?
A. iron oxide
B. red paint
C. tomato soup

4 What is Jupiter's Great Red Spot?
A. a huge volcano
B. a really big pimple
C. a giant storm

5 What are Saturn's rings made of?
A. cotton candy
B. ice and rock
C. silk

6 Why do astronomers think Uranus is tipped on its side?
A. something big once crashed into it
B. it's too lazy to stand up straight
C. the sun's gravity knocked it over

7 What shoots out of Saturn's moon Enceladus?
A. lava
B. chocolate
C. ice crystals

8 What do you call a planet that orbits a different star?
A. outer planet
B. extra planet
C. exoplanet

GLOSSARY

asteroid a large chunk of rock left over from when the planets formed

astronomer person who studies the sun, the moon, the planets, and the stars

atmosphere a layer of gas trapped by gravity around the surface of a planet or moon

axis an imaginary line through the middle of a planet or moon that it spins around

carbon dioxide a heavy colorless gas

core the center of a planet or moon

crater circular hole made when a comet, asteroid, or meteorite hits a planet or moon

dwarf planet object that is too small to be considered a planet, but too big to be an asteroid

exoplanet planet that orbits a star other than the sun

gravity a force that pulls objects together. The heavier or closer an object is, the stronger its gravity, or pull.

ice cap a thick layer of ice that covers the ground. Some planets have ice caps at their poles.

lava melted rock that pours onto a planet's surface from underground

light-year the distance that light can travel in one year

mass the measure of the amount of material in an object

moon object that orbits a planet or asteroid

orbit the path an object takes around a larger object; or, to take such a path

solar system a group of planets that circles a star

solar wind stream of electrified gas that flies out of the Sun and across space at very a high speed

telescope tool used for studying space, which gathers information about things that are far away

temperature measure of how hot or cold something is

volcano mountain formed from lava that erupts onto the surface from underground

FURTHER RESOURCES

Books

Aguilar, David A. *13 Planets: The Latest View of the Solar System.* Washington, DC: National Geographic Kids, 2011.

Berger, Melvin. *Discovering Mars: The Amazing Story of the Red Planet.* New York: Scholastic, 2015.

Mist, Rosalind. *The Solar System.* Minneapolis, MN: QEB Publishing, 2014.

Simon, Seymour. *Our Solar System.* New York: HarperCollins, 2014.

Solar System. DK Findout! New York: Dorling Kindersley, 2016.

Websites

For web resources related
to the subject of this book, go to:
www.windmillbooks.com/weblinks
and select this book's title.

INDEX

Answers to quiz:
1. b; 2. a; 3. a; 4. c; 5. b; 6. a; 7. c; 8. c